CONTENTS

PREFACE

The Law Society business lease has been published, in two versions, by the Law Society to provide a ready for use standard form of lease for certain business properties which holds a reasonably fair balance between the parties. This Companion is intended to provide users with immediate references to the general rules which lie behind the drafting of the lease, some guidance to the effect of its terms and a number of suggestions for extra clauses which would give effect to possible amendments or additions.

Use of lease

The lease should prove useful for fairly short lettings — perhaps up to ten years — of relatively modest properties; it was not designed to be used for all leases of business premises. It does not provide terms likely to prove acceptable to financial institutions funding major property developments or investments, but there are of course many properties which would not be acceptable to them either. On the other hand, it appears to cover, in a much simpler style than is customary, all the essential points which are likely to be needed for a routine letting.

Two versions

The lease is published in two versions: one for letting a whole building and the other for letting only part of a building. The latter version has extra terms in it which are necessitated by the fact that the property let is only part of a building. So, there are provisions for services to be supplied by the landlord and a service charge paid by the tenant to contribute towards the cost of them. Also, it has terms to settle where the boundaries between the property let and the rest of the building lie and to provide for the necessary easements.

The additional terms in the 'part of building' version mean that equivalent clauses in the two versions are often differently numbered. This Companion adopts the convention of referring to clauses in the lease of part of a building in italics, eg *3.2*.

Residential use

The version of the lease adapted for letting whole buildings makes optional provision for the use of part of the property as a residence. A shop with a flat above, let together as one building, is an obvious example of the situation that this would cover. If there is no residential use, the only adaptation required is to delete the provisions for describing the residential accommodation in the initial definition clause on the front page of the lease.

Even if the letting is partly for residential purposes, the special legislative provisions protecting residential tenants will not apply because, being a business letting, this will be a tenancy to which the Landlord and Tenant Act 1954, Pt II, applies. (*See* Landlord and Tenant Acts 1985, s 32, and 1987, s 46(1) and Housing Act 1988, Sch 1, para 4.)

Amendments

Naturally, users may from time to time wish to amend the standard lease terms. While there is no restriction on doing so, the Law Society is anxious that the standard terms should be reproduced as published, with amendments being made by reference on attached sheets. This serves the important purpose of not concealing minor but significant amendments in the printed text; they can only be a trap for the user. However if amendments appear at the end, familiarity with the standard form will make using it quick and easy without repetitive re-reading, and changes for a particular occasion will be highlighted.

A number of possible additional clauses, either amending or supplementing the standard terms, are given at the end of the Companion with a brief explanation of each. These additional clauses are intended for use with the lease, being drafted in a similar plain style and sometimes cross-referring to the standard clauses.

Companion to the Law Society Business Lease

TENANT'S OBLIGATIONS

Payments

1.1 No special method of payment of rent is specified. One possible method is by banker's order (see Additional Clause **A**).

1.2 The sums payable to the landlord — the amount of the insurance premium (*whole building*) and the service charge (*part of building*) — are 'to be paid as rent'. This is often assumed to have two effects: first, if there are arrears no notice need be served as a preliminary to forfeiture (Law of Property Act 1925, s 146(11)); secondly, the landlord will be able to distrain for arrears. Neither of these consequences is certain. Section 146 does not apply in the case of nonpayment of 'rent', but it is not certain that whatever the parties deem to be rent can be similarly excluded. As to distress, the right may not be exercisable in respect of all payments normally treated as rent (see *United Scientific Holdings Ltd* v *Burnley Borough Council* [1978] AC 904, 947); where the tenant is an individual the Bills of Sale Acts will make any extension of the right unenforceable.

1.3 The surveyor nominated by the landlord must be truly separate from the landlord (*Finchbourne Ltd* v *Rodrigues* [1976] 3 All ER 581). He acts in an arbitral capacity and must not simply follow the landlord's instructions. The landlord's managing agent will not normally be a suitable nominee (*Concorde Graphics Ltd* v *Andromeda Investments SA* (1982) 265 EG 386).

1.4 The landlord is given power to do work to the property on the tenant's default by clause **5.5(c)** (**6.8(c)**) and has an express right of access for that purpose under clause **4.1(b)** (**5.1(b)**).

1.5   (*a*)   Only if, as here, a lease imposes an obligation does the tenant have to pay the costs incurred by the landlord when the tenant applies for a consent (*Goldman* v *Abbott* [1989] 2 EGLR 78).

       (*b*)   The landlord's right to claim costs when a lease is not forfeited only applies where relief is granted under the Act (Law of

Property Act 1925, s 146(3); this clause extends the tenant's obligation.

(c) Serving a schedule of dilapidations at the end of the term, to quantify a claim for breach of clause **13.1** (*15.1*), is not subject to section 146 because any proceedings would not be for the premature ending of a term by forfeiture; terms relating to the costs of such a notice do not, therefore, apply and separate provision is needed.

1.6 The current figure for the Law Society's interest rate is published in each issue of the *Law Society's Gazette*.

(*a*) Even though the lease purports to preclude deductions from rent etc, those authorised by statute can still be made. Examples are: income tax at the basic rate on rent payable to a landlord whose usual place of abode is outside the UK (Income and Corporation Taxes Act 1988, s 43); rent paid by a subtenant to a head landlord (*O'Donoghue* v *Coalbrook and Broadoak Co Ltd* (1872) 26 LT 806); statutory compensation for improvements which the landlord owed to the tenant (Landlord and Tenant Act 1927, s 11(2)). In the absence of the agreement to the contrary which the lease includes, the tenant has a right of equitable set-off for sums arising under the same lease or a closely connected contract.

(*b*) All sums payable under the lease are assumed to be exclusive of value added tax. They are therefore payable together with tax at the current rate, even if the rate has increased, or tax has been charged on something previously not taxed, since the lease was granted (Value Added Tax Act 1983, s 42).

2.1 'Rates' will cover non-domestic rates and the few remaining special local rates. 'Taxes' generally refer only to those imposed by Parliament. 'Outgoings' is a term of very wide scope (*Smith* v *Smith* [1939] 4 All ER 212); it has been held to cover non-recurring capital items, but will not do so here because it is qualified by 'periodic'. The inclusion of new impositions of a novel nature, catches property based charges for which the tenant would not otherwise be liable (*Mile End Old Town Vestry* v *Whitby* (1898) 78 LT 80).

2.2 Clause **3.8** (*4.8*) makes the tenant responsible for ensuring that any licence to conduct the business, or registration of the property for that purpose, is obtained and kept up to date.

2.3 Clause **6.4** (*7.4*) obliges the tenant to register every transfer, mortgage and sublease. With VAT at 17.5%, £23.50 is payable in respect of each document, even if more than one is registered at the same time.

Service charge
The lease of part of building assumes that the whole of

2

the premises let will be put to business use and therefore makes no provision for including terms relating to residential accommodation. Accordingly, it is assumed that the statutory restrictions on service charges payable in respect of dwellings (Landlord and Tenant Act 1985, ss 18–30, amended by Landlord and Tenant Act 1987) do not apply.

3.1 'Fair proportion' is not defined. The test is to be applied to each item of service charge costs, so the share which one tenant pays may vary from item to item of the costs, depending upon what degree he relies on a particular service. This could lead to burdensome calculations, which might vary with each payment; a possible variation would adopt a single percentage fixed at the outset (see Additional Clause **B**).

3.2 (*a*) The landlord cannot include in the service charge anything spent on items not specified in clauses *12* or *13* (*Riverlate Properties Ltd v Paul* [1975] Ch 133). The restriction on the amount of the landlord's expenditure repaid by the service charge to what is 'fair and reasonable' reflects the common law (*Firstcross Ltd v Teasdale* (1982) 265 EG 305). 'Costs' has been held not to include interest on money borrowed by the landlord (*Boldmark Ltd v Cohen* [1986] 1 EGLR 47), but see (*c*) below.

  (*b*) The reasonableness of a management charge made by a landlord's holding company has been assessed by making a comparison with what an independent managing agent would have charged (*Parkside Knightsbridge Ltd v Horwitz* (1983) 268 EG 49).

  (*c*) The cost of borrowing money to finance the provision of services can only be included in a service charge if expressly authorised (*Frobisher Second Investments Ltd v Kiloran Trust Co Ltd* [1980] 1 WLR 425). For the Law Society's interest rate see **1.6** above.

3.3 For the tenant's obligation to pay, see clause **1.2**. Interest on overdue payments is payable under clause **1.6**.

3.4, *3.5* The ability to collect interim payments for future expenditure is important because lack of money does not excuse a breach of a duty to provide a service (*Francis v Cowcliff Ltd* (1976) 33 P&CR 368).

3.6 The time limit for the landlord to demand a service charge is not strictly enforced (*West Central Investments Ltd v Borovik* (1976) 241 EG 609).

3.7 For the tenant's obligation to pay, see clause **1.2**. Interest on overdue payments is payable under clause **1.6**. Overpayments may only be retained by the landlord towards demands made for interim payments, which cannot occur once the lease ends.

3.8, —

3.9

Use

3 (*4*) A tenant who did not prevent someone else from doing something he could have prevented has been held to 'permit' that act (*Norton* v *Charles Deane Productions Ltd* [1970] EGD 268). Presumably the same interpretation would apply to 'allow'.

3.1 (*4.1*) This is framed as a positive obligation, requiring the tenant to use the premises for the specified purpose. Allowing the premises to remain unused would be a breach of covenant. The 'use allowed' is to be defined in the initial definitions clause.

3.2 In another context (qualification as a secure tenancy: Housing Act 1985, s 81) 'occupation as a home' was held not to require full-time physical occupation (*Crawley Borough Council* v *Sawyer* (1988) 20 HLR 98).

4.2 The tenant's authority to use rights of way for access is granted by clause *16.2*.

3.3 (*4.3*) The landlord is under a duty to give the tenant particulars of the insurance policy on request (see clause **11.3** (*12.3*)), so he can obtain the information necessary to comply with the policy terms.

3.4 (*4.4*) —

3.5 (*4.5*) There can be no precise definition of what is dangerous, offensive or noxious. Surrounding circumstances must be taken into account. Illegal use includes one for which planning consent has been refused (*Best* v *Glenville* [1960] 1 WLR 1198). Immoral use seems to be interpreted according to the ideas of the times (letting a flat to a man for his mistress, was immoral: *Upfill* v *Wright* [1911] 1 KB 506; but now probably not: *Heglibiston Establishments* v *Heyman* (1977) 76 P&CR 351). 'Nuisance' bears its technical meaning in the law of tort but 'annoyance' is wider (*Tod-Heatly* v *Benham* (1888) 40 ChD 80).

3.6 (*4.6*) For planning purposes, words on a shop blind were held to be an advertisement (*Westminster City Council* v *Secretary of State for the Environment* (1989) 59 P&CR 496). Once the landlord gives consent, he cannot later withdraw it unless he originally reserves the right to do so (*William Hill (Southern) Ltd* v *Cabras Ltd* (1985) 275 EG 149).

3.7 (*4.7*) —

3.8 (*4.8*) Even though the tenant, independently of the lease, has an obligation to comply with statutory and other requirements, and there are sanctions if he is in breach, the inclusion of an express covenant gives

4

the landlord the chance to forfeit rather than wait for an outside authority to take enforcement measures (eg *Ali v Booth* (1966) 110 SJ 708: offences against regulations under the Food and Drugs Act 1955). This clause covers compliance with town and country planning measures, which leases often treat separately.

Access

4 (*5*)   A landlord has no right of access to the property which he lets unless the right is reserved, whether expressly, by implication or by statute (*Stocker* v *Planet Building Society* (1879) 27 WR 877; *Plough Investments Ltd* v *Manchester City Council* [1989] 1 EGLR 244, 248).

4.1 (*5.1*)   —

4.2 (*5.2*)   As to the service of notices, see clause **14.4** (***17.4***).

4.3 (*5.3*)   —

4.4 (*5.4*)   Because the access right is granted on terms that the landlord pay for any damage, once he exercises the right the landlord assumes the obligation to pay the tenant (*Halsall* v *Brizell* [1957] Ch 169).

Condition

5.1 (*6.1*)   The lease does not contain a conventional repairing clause. While the obligation to 'maintain' a building may be analogous to a duty to repair it (*ACT Construction Ltd* v *Customs and Excise Commissioners* [1981] 1 WLR 1542), that is not how the word is used here. It is the state and condition which is to be maintained, which is to preserve the status quo, in other words, 'to preserve [that state] unimpaired' (*Shorter Oxford Dictionary*). Where only part of the building is let, this obligation is confined to the inside of the property, see **6.6** below.

5.2 (*6.2*)   The obligation to decorate 'in every fifth year of the lease period' arises at the beginning of that year, so it is effective even if the lease ends during the year (*Kirklinton* v *Wood* [1917] 1 KB 332). For a clause to change the specified years for redecoration, see Additional Clause **C**. The reference to 'the last three months' would apply to the last three months of the original period, ignoring premature termination, were it not for the insertion of 'however it ends' (*Dickinson* v *St Aubyn* [1944] KB 454).

6.3   The obligation to 'maintain' a shop front probably amounts to a duty to repair it (compare *6.1* above). Note the restrictions on the colours to be used, clause *6.4*.

6.4   —

5.3 (*6.5*)   The tenant's duty to comply with statutory requirements is qualified, as far as his obligation to the landlord is concerned, by the exclusion of alterations and improvements (clause **5.2**, **6.7**). If he is nevertheless obliged by the statute to do the work, there are cases in which he may be able to shift the burden of some or all of the cost to the landlord: for example, shops and offices (Offices Shops and Railway Premises Act 1963, s 13(4), (5)), factories (Factories Act 1961, s 28), entertainment and eating premises (Local Government (Miscellaneous Provisions) Act 1976, ss 20, 21), fire safety work (Fire Precautions Act 1971, s 9A(2); Fire Safety and Safety of Places of Sport Act 1987, s 5).

6.6   This clause does not define the boundaries of the property let (see clause **16.1**), but merely the extent of the tenant's obligations in relation to condition. If the premises have a false ceiling, both ceilings may be included (*Graystone Property Investments Ltd* v *Margulies* (1983) 269 EG 538).

5.4 (*6.7*)

(*a*)   'Improvement' is a narrower term than 'altera-tion'. Whether work is an improvement is to be considered from the tenant's point of view (*Lambert* v *F W Woolworth & Co Ltd (No 2)* [1938] Ch 883). An alteration may be limited to work which physically changes the structure, rather than merely attaching something to it (*Bickmore* v *Dimmer* [1903] 1 Ch 158).

(*b*)   Unless there is an express qualification to exclude liability for damage which has been insured, the tenant is still liable to reinstate the property (*Manchester Bonded Warehouse Co* v *Carr* (1880) 5 CPD 507, 513).

5.5 (*6.8*)   Without authority in the lease, the landlord cannot do work on the property even if the tenant should have done it but has not (*Regional Properties Ltd* v *City of London Real Property Co Ltd*; *Sedgwick Forbes Bland Payne Group Ltd* v *Regional Properties Ltd* (1981) 257 EG 257). A landlord who enters without authority and does the work cannot recover the cost of it (*Hamilton* v *Martell Securities Ltd* [1984] Ch 266, 282).

5.6 (*6.9*)   A tenant who proposes to improve the property (here, in the sense that its letting value is increased) can in most cases override the lease terms and the landlord's objections by applying to court. That is only when the improvement is reasonable and suitable to the character of the property and does not diminish the value of other property belonging to the landlord (Landlord and Tenant Act 1927, s 3). As the prohibition is limited to structural alterations, some acts which have in the past been breaches of wider covenants might not be caught: eg, raising a parapet wall in breach of a covenant not to alter the plan layout height or elevation of the premises (*Viscount Chelsea* v *Muscatt* [1990] 2 EGLR 48); converting a house into five flats in contravention of a covenant against altering internal planning (*Eyre* v *Rea* [1947] KB 567).

5.7 (*6.10*) The tenant may apply to the court for a declaration that the landlord is acting unreasonably in withholding consent (Landlord and Tenant Act 1954, s 53). The onus of proof is on the tenant, unless the landlord has offered no explanation. The possibility of disturbance to the landlord is not a major factor (*Haines* v *Florensa* (1990) 59 P&CR 200).

5.8 (*6.11*) —

Transfer etc

6.1 (*7.1*) A major reason for placing an unconditional ban on dealings with part only of the property is that every tenant in occupation for business purposes enjoys statutory renewal rights (Landlord and Tenant Act 1954, s 23), so that allowing it to be divided may result (subject to the operation of s 32(2)) in the landlord being faced with the management problems associated with a multiplicity of tenants.

6.2 (*7.2*) The landlord has a duty to give consent when it is reasonable to do so, to give it within a reasonable time and to give the tenant notice of his decision (Landlord and Tenant Act 1988, s 1). The landlord's discretion allows him to withhold consent to prevent his property being used or occupied in an undesirable way or by an undesirable person, but his grounds must relate to the landlord and tenant relationship concerning that property. The landlord's conclusions need not be justified if they could have been reached by a reasonable man (*International Drilling Fluids Ltd* v *Louisville Investments (Uxbridge) Ltd* [1986] Ch 513, 519–20). Some flexibility can be added to the position of a tenant company by freely allowing transfers within the tenant's group of companies, see Additional Clause **D**.

6.3 (*7.3*) Even if a sublease purports to authorise a use of the property which the head lease forbids, the subtenant can be stopped from using it in that way (*Hill* v *Harris* [1965] 2 QB 601).

6.4 (*7.4*) —

Other matters

7.1 (*8.1*) A notice may relate to proposed action under statutory powers which would affect the landlord's long-term interest in the property.

7.2 (*8.2*) —

7.3 (*8.3*) Because a material change in the use of property requires planning permission (Town and Country Planning Act 1990, s 55(1)), if the tenant obtains and implements a consent to change the use, the landlord may be faced with the need for permission to revert to the former use.

8.1 (*9.1*)   Rent review dates are defined in the initial definitions clause. This is an 'upwards only' review, but not if the parties agree that a review should be able to go down, see Additional Clause **E**.

8.2 (*9.2*)   The basis on which the new rent is to be assessed is set out, but points which are not dealt with will follow the current terms of the lease (*Basingstoke and Deane Borough Council* v *Host Group Ltd* [1988] 1 WLR 348, 354). This is a letting by a willing landlord to a willing tenant, meaning hypothetical parties without the attributes of the actual landlord and tenant (*FR Evans (Leeds) Ltd* v *English Electric Co Ltd* (1979) 36 P&CR 185). Granting a new lease means that the value of fixtures which the tenant could remove is ignored (*New Zealand Property Corporation* v *HM & S Ltd* [1982] QB 1145). The assumption that the term is what remains of the lease period at the review date follows the general law (*Norwich Union Life Assurance Society* v *Trustee Savings Bank Central Board* [1986] 1 EGLR 136).

(*a*)   The possibility of a statutory extension will normally be taken into account (*Pivot Properties Ltd* v *Secretary of State for the Environment* (1980) 41 P&CR 248). Disregarding goodwill follows the rent fixing formula on a lease renewal (Landlord and Tenant Act 1954, s 34(1)(*b*)).

(*b*)   The assumption that the property is vacant may, in an appropriate case, reduce the new rent by giving a discount to represent a rent free initial period (*No 99 Bishopsgate Ltd* v *Prudential Assurance Co Ltd* [1985] 1 EGLR 72).

(*c*)   The assumption that the property can immediately be used presumably means both that it is physically adapted for the purpose (reversing the effect of *Trust House Forte Albany Hotels Ltd* v *Daejan Investments Ltd* (1980) 265 EG 915) and that the use is permitted for planning purposes (*Bovis Group Pension Fund Ltd* v *GC Furnishing and Flooring Ltd* (1984) 269 EG 1252).

(*d*)   The property is valued as it stands, ignoring dilapidations which are the tenant's responsibility (*Harmsworth Pension Funds Trustees Ltd* v *Charrington Industrial Holdings Ltd* (1985) 49 P&CR 297).

(*e*)   Any improvements to the property made by the tenant are to be ignored (reversing the effect of *Ponsford* v *HMS Aerosols* [1979] AC 63).

8.3 (*9.3*)   If necessary, a memorandum recording the

result of a review can be rectified (*Equity & Law Life Assurance Society Ltd* v *Coltness Group Ltd* (1983) 267 EG 949).

8.4 (*9.4*)   Time is not of the essence for applying for the appointment of an arbitrator (*Metrolands Investments Ltd* v *JH Dewhurst Ltd* [1986] 3 All ER 659).

8.5 (*9.5*)

(*a*)   —

(*b*)   Payment of the new rent starts on the rent day next following settlement of the figure (*South Tottenham Land Securities Ltd* v *R & A Millett (Shops) Ltd* [1984] 1 WLR 710).

(*c*)   Backdating of the new rent is effective (*CH Bailey Ltd* v *Memorial Enterprises Ltd* [1974] 1 WLR 728). If interest is to be payable, the lease must specify this (*Trust House Forte Albany Hotels Ltd* v *Daejan Investments Ltd* (1980) 256 EG 915). For the Law Society's interest rate, see **1.6** above. If the lease has changed hands, the backdated rent is the liability of the person who was the tenant for the time being (*Parry* v *Robinson-Wylie* [1987] 2 EGLR 133).

DAMAGE

9 (*10*)   Risks to be insured: see clause 11.1(*b*) (*12.1(b)*). Common parts: see clause **13.1(*b*)**.

9.1 (*10.1*)   Without an express provision in the lease, damage by an insured risk does not suspend the duty to pay rent (*Matthey* v *Curling* [1922] 2 AC 180).

9.2 (*10.2*)   The landlord's right to end the lease is subject to the tenant's renewal rights under the Landlord and Tenant Act 1954, Pt II. The fact that property is rendered unusable by fire, so that the tenant has to cease to trade there, does not necessarily prevent his claiming the right to renew (*Morrison Holdings Ltd* v *Manders Property (Wolverhampton) Ltd* [1976] 1 WLR 767). If the tenant gives notice, the lease will end and the tenant will not have the right to renew, provided that when the notice is given, he has been in occupation under the tenancy for at least one month (Landlord and Tenant Act 1954, s 24(2)(*a*)).

9.3 (*10.3*)   Time is of the essence for giving notice under clause **9.2 (*10.2*)**.

9.4 (*10.4*)   —

LANDLORD'S OBLIGATIONS AND FORFEITURE RIGHTS

Quiet enjoyment

10 (*11*)   This covenant supersedes the implied covenant for quiet enjoyment (*Miller* v *Emcer Products Ltd* [1956] Ch 304). The landlord's responsibility is qualified; he is not responsible for the eviction of the tenant by a head landlord for non-payment of the head rent (*Kelly* v *Rogers* [1892] 1 QB 910) or because the head lease was not of sufficient length to grant a sublease for the term which he purported to grant (*Baynes & Co* v *Lloyd & Sons* [1895] 2 QB 610). Nor is the landlord responsible for the acts of his predecessor in title (*Celsteel Ltd* v *Alton House Holdings Ltd (No 2)* [1987] 1 WLR 291) or the tenant under a previous lease to which he was not a party (*Re Griffiths, Griffiths* v *Riggs* (1917) 61 SJ 268).

Insurance

12.1 (*13.1*) The amount of insurance cover should include an allowance for likely inflation during the rebuilding period and the time that the necessary preliminaries can be expected to take (*Glennifer Finance Corporation* v *Bamar Wood & Products Ltd* (1978) 37 P&CR 208). A landlord cannot add risks, other than those specified, to the insurance and charge the premium to the tenant unless he is expressly authorised to do so (*Upjohn* v *Hitchens* [1918] 2 KB 48). The insurance obligation is limited to the extent that cover is available to protect the landlord; if he had a duty to insure fully and full cover was not available, he would have to make up any shortfall in the amount recovered (*Enlayde Ltd* v *Roberts* [1917] 1 Ch 109). On a letting of a whole building, the tenant reimburses the amount of the insurance premium (clause **1.2**), when a service charge is payable the landlord's cost of complying with his insurance obligations is part of the service costs (clause *3.2*).

Services

13 The cost of providing the services listed is a service cost, a proportion of which goes to make up the service charge payable by the tenant (clause *3.2*). The cost of work contracted for during the lease period, but not actually done until afterwards, will not be included (*Capital & Counties Freehold Equity Trust Ltd* v *BL plc* [1987] 2 EGLR 49).

The exclusion of liability, at the end of the clause, may be subject to some qualifications. The fact that plant wears out, so that it can no longer function to provide a service, is not 'beyond the control of the landlord' (*Yorkbrook Investments Ltd* v *Batten* (1985) 276 EG 545). Managing agents who were negligent in recruiting porters were liable when one stole from a tenant's premises (*Nahhas* v *Pier House (Cheyne Walk) Management Ltd* (1984) 270 EG 328). The Unfair Contract Terms Act 1977 restricts or excludes the possibility of limiting liability for negligence in certain cases. How far it applies here is uncertain, because its principal operative provisions do not apply to 'any contract so far as it relates to the creation . . . of an interest in land' (Sch 1, para 1(*b*)). Clearly, a lease does create an interest in land; but do service charge relate to that aspect of it?

13.1 For the nature of the obligation to maintain, see **5.1** above. So long as he bears in mind the extent of the duty, it is for the landlord to determine the standard and nature of the work which is undertaken. Within reason, he can decide to do a permanent and more costly job instead of a cheaper but temporary one (*Manor House Drive Ltd* v *Shahbazian* (1965) 195 EG 283).

13.2 The five year decorating cycle for the common parts and the outside of the building is not linked to the date of the grant of the lease, ie it is not the same as in every fifth year of the lease period. The tenant will therefore have an obligation to contribute even if the decoration is done very shortly after his arrival. For common parts, see clause ***13.1(b)***.

13.3 *See* **2.1** above.

13.4 —

13.5 The list of services at the end of the lease should be adapted to apply to the building in question. However deleting some will not necessarily remove liability. The landlord will, for example, be liable under his duty of care to provide adequate lighting on stairs which remain in his occupation as part of the common parts (*Huggett* v *Miers* [1908] 2 KB 278). The landlord should consider whether to refer to the services in general terms (eg 'porterage') or to be more specific (eg '24 hour protection from independent security guard contractors'), because he cannot charge more than the cost of the most economical way of providing any specified service (*Russell* v *Laimond Properties Ltd* (1984) 269 EG 947).

Forfeiture

12 (*14*)

(*a*) The clause dispenses with the need for a formal demand for rent before forfeiture on the ground of non-payment which otherwise applies (*Doe d Harris* v *Masters* (1824) 2 B&C 490).

(*b*) —

(*c*) Insolvency of an individual, as a ground for forfeiture, relates only to the tenant. If the landlord wishes to extend it to the guarantor's insolvency, see Additional Clause **F**. In the latter case, notice under the Law of Property Act 1925 s 146 would still be necessary as a preliminary to forfeiture (*Halliard Property Co Ltd* v *Jack Segal Ltd* [1978] 1 WLR 377). Interim receiver, see Insolvency Act 1986, s 286.

(*d*) Administrative receiver, see Insolvency Act 1986, s 29(2); administration order see 1986 Act, s 8.

END OF LEASE

13.1 (*15.1*)   This clause imposes two obligations on the tenant. The first is to yield the property up to the landlord at the end of the lease period. This requires him to ensure that any subtenant has quit (*Thames Manufacturing Co Ltd* v *Parrotts (Nichol & Payton) Ltd* (1984) 128 SJ 447). It also means that if there is a default, any guarantor is liable for damages for the landlord's resulting loss (*Associated Dairies Ltd* v *Pierce* (1982) 265 EG 127). Secondly, the property must be in a state and condition complying with clause **5** (*6*), and in default the landlord will be able to claim damages for dilapidations.

13.2 (*15.2*)   In the absence of any requirement by the landlord under this clause, the position is that the tenant has a duty to remove his furniture (*Norwich Union Life Assurance Society* v *Preston* [1957] 1 WLR 813) and rubbish (*Cumberland Consolidated Holdings Ltd* v *Ireland* [1946] 2 KB 264). In addition, he has a right to remove tenant's fixtures, but if he does not they become the landlord's property (*Smith* v *City Petroleum Co Ltd* [1940] 1 All ER 260). When a fixture is lawfully removed, any damage to the fabric of the property which had been made to accommodate the fixture in the first place must be repaired (*Mancetter Developments Ltd* v *Garmanson Ltd* [1986] QB 1212).

PROPERTY RIGHTS

Boundaries

16.1   Without special provision, the external surfaces of the outside walls would be included in the demise of the property, notwithstanding that the landlord has the duty to repair them (*Sturge* v *Hackett* [1962] 1 WLR 1257).

Facilities

16.2   Where appropriate the right of access will presumably include using a lift, as that can constitute an easement (*Liverpool City Council* v *Irwin* [1977] AC 239). However, there cannot be an easement for protection from the weather (*Phipps* v *Pears* [1965] 1 QB 76). A tenant whose lease granted him the use of private forecourts and roadways was held entitled to park without payment (*Papworth* v *Linthaven Ltd* [1988] EGCS 54). It seems unlikely that the landlord's right, under this lease to make reasonable rules, would extend to imposing a charge for parking.

16.3   The rights for the landlord are probably correctly interpreted as a reservation, in which case the rights may be validly reserved not only to the landlord but also to third parties, eg his tenants (*Woodward* v *Haywood* (1910) 27 TLR 123). The practical significance is that if the reservation is directly in favour of third parties they will be able to enforce their rights.

GENERAL

Parties' Responsibility

14.1 (*17.1*)　Covenants by more than one person impose joint responsibility, rather than joint and several, unless there is express provision to the contrary (*White* v *Tyndall* (1888) 13 App Cas 263). One joint party, against whom a covenant is enforced, can recover a contribution from the other(s) (Civil Liability (Contribution) Act 1978, s 3). The original parties to a lease normally remain liable under their covenants through the term, even though they have parted with all interest in the property. A term of the lease can cancel that liability, see Additional Clause **G**.

Landlord

14.2 (*17.2*)　Where the lease is granted for a fixed term of more than one year or for a term of years and thereafter from year to year, the tenant can serve notice on a prescribed form to obtain details of the ownership of superior interests (Landlord and Tenant Act 1954, s 40(2)).

Tenant

14.3 (*17.3*)　The landlord may serve notice in a prescribed form on the tenant to obtain details of his occupation and the identity of subtenants (Landlord and Tenant Act 1954, s 40(1)). A solicitor taking action on behalf of a tenant will normally have a duty to divulge his client's name on request (*Pascall* v *Galinski* [1970] 1 QB 38, 44).

Service of notices

14.4 (*17.4*)　The Law of Property Act 1925, s 196 (as amended) requires all notices to be in writing. It authorises service on a tenant by addressing a notice to 'the lessee' or even to 'the persons interested'. Notices may be left at the addressee's last known place of abode or business in the UK, or, in the case of one for the tenant, be left at the property. Notices may be sent by post, registered or recorded delivery, addressed to the addressee by name. They are deemed to have been served when they would in the ordinary course have been delivered, unless returned undelivered. Advantage can be taken of other statutory provisions, for example a company may be served by sending a notice to its registered office or leaving it there (Companies Act 1985, s 725). In any event, if the addressee received the notice, there is good service (*Stylo Shoes Ltd* v *Prices Tailors Ltd* [1960] Ch 396).

Arbitration

14.5 (*17.5*) The Arbitration Act 1950 makes automatic provision for a number of matters sometimes expressly dealt with in leases: the arbitrator refuses to act, is incapable of doing so or dies (s 10(*b*)), witnesses and evidence (s 11), interim and final awards (ss 13, 14), costs (s 18), interest (s 20).

Headings

14.6 (*17.6*) —

GUARANTEE BOX

If the lease is extended under the Landlord and Tenant Act 1954, the guarantor's liability continues into the extension period (contrary the conclusion reached in *Junction Estates Ltd* v *Cope* (1974) 24 P&CR 482). Even after the surrender of a lease, a guarantor continues to be liable for the tenant's obligations incurred before the surrender (*Torminster Properties Ltd* v *Green* [1983] 1 WLR 676). On an application to renew the lease, the guarantor cannot be obliged to guarantee the tenant's obligations under the lease, but the court may agree that the lease should contain a term that the tenant must produce an acceptable guarantor within a specified period (*Cairnplace Ltd* v *CBL (Property Investment) Co Ltd* [1984] 1 WLR 696).

Additional Clauses

The published forms of lease are intended to be used without the text being amended, but to be adapted as necessary by adding special terms on extra sheets to draw attention to variations. The following possible additions are suggested to deal with points made in the foregoing comments on particular clauses.

Payment of rent

   A The Tenant is to make all payments of rent by banker's order as from time to time directed by the Landlord

Although theoretically a tenant is under an obligation to volunteer payments of rent, in the same way as any debtor must pay a sum due, the accepted practice is to send a rent demand for each instalment. Payment by banker's order avoids that, although the landlord will still need to check that the money has been received. A banker's order is not suitable for the payment of service charge, because the sums vary. A variable amount direct debit could be used, but it is doubtful whether it would be acceptable to a tenant.

Service charge

   B For the purpose of clauses 3.1 and 3.4, a fair proportion is . . . per cent

This is for cases where it is more convenient to have a service charge which is a fixed proportion of the underlying costs. The same percentage is adopted both for the total service charge and for interim payments. A landlord who adopts this clause will normally wish to use it for all parts of the building which are let.

Year to decorate

   C The Tenant's duty to decorate under clause 5.2(*a*) [*6.2(a)*] applies only in the . . . [and . . .] year[s] of the lease period

The standard decorating interval, every fifth year, may be unsuitable. For example, if the letting is for six years paragraphs (*a*) and (*b*) of clause **5.2** would together require decoration in successive years.

Assignment within group of companies

   D Notwithstanding clause 6.2 [7.2], the Tenant may at any time transfer the whole property to any company of which it is a subsidiary or which is its subsidiary (within the meaning of section 736(1) of the Companies Act 1985)

This allows the free assignment of the lease within a group of companies; the obligation to give notice of any transfer (clause **6.4** (*7.4*)) would continue to apply.

Upwards or downwards rent review

E   Clause 8.1 is to be varied to read: 'On each rent review date, the rent is to be adjusted to the market rent', and any reference in this lease to an increase of rent is to be read as a reference to an adjustment of it

Although upwards only rent reviews are the most common, there is no legal presumption that a review should operate in that way (*Philpots (Woking) Ltd* v *Surrey Conveyancers Ltd* [1986] 1 EGLR 97).

Insolvency of surety

F   Clause 12(c) [14(c)] shall apply in relation to the Guarantor as it does in relation to the Tenant

This clause makes the insolvency of the Guarantor a ground for forfeiting the lease, in the same way as the insolvency of the tenant.

Original parties' liability

G   The original tenant and the original landlord (named above) is, respectively, only liable for breaches of the obligations in this lease which occur while he retains his interest in the property

The original parties to a lease normally continue to be liable under the lease covenants throughout the term, by privity of contract, even if the lease terms are varied (*Selous Street Properties Ltd* v *Oronel Fabrics Ltd* (1984) 270 EG 643). This clause cancels that liability for breaches after they have transferred their interest.

Excluding renewal

H   Sections 24 to 28 of the Landlord and Tenant Act 1954 do not apply to this lease

To exclude the tenant's right to renew a business lease it is necessary to obtain the court's approval in advance and to have a term to this effect in the lease (1954 Act, s 38(4)).

Excluding compensation

I   The Tenant is not entitled to compensation under section 37 of the Landlord and Tenant Act 1954

The tenant's statutory right to compensation, if refused a renewal of his lease on certain grounds, can be excluded unless the tenant and his predecessor(s) in business had been carrying on business there continuously for at least five years (1954 Act, s 38(2), (3)). A lease can properly include a term excluding the right to compensation for use if, on the facts as they exist when it ends, it proves to be valid.

Costs of the lease

J When this lease is granted, the Tenant is to pay the landlord the expenses which he incurred in connection with negotiating and granting it, amounting to £. . . (including value added tax)

Where there is no formal preliminary agreement for the grant of the lease and the tenant has accepted responsibility for the landlord's costs, the landlord will generally obtain payment by simply requiring the money before the grant is completed. However, a lease term may be convenient as a way to ensure that this term is indeed part of the bargain.

Table of Equivalent Clauses

Whole building	Part of building
TENANT'S OBLIGATIONS	
Payments	
1	*1*
1.1	*1.1*
1.2	*1.2*
1.3	*1.3*
1.4	*1.4*
1.5	*1.5*
1.6	*1.6*
2	*2*
2.1	*2.1*
2.2	*2.2*
2.3	*2.3*
	Service charge
—	*3*
—	*3.1*
—	*3.2*
—	*3.3*
—	*3.4*
—	*3.5*
—	*3.6*
—	*3.7*
—	*3.8*
—	*3.9*
Use	
3	*4*
3.1	*4.1*
3.2	—
—	*4.2*
3.3	*4.3*
3.4	*4.4*
3.5	*4.5*
3.6	*4.6*
3.7	*4.7*
3.8	*4.8*
Access	
4	*5*
4.1	*5.1*
4.2	*5.2*
4.3	*5.3*
4.4	*5.4*
Condition	
5	*6*
5.1	*6.1*
5.2, part	*6.2*
—	*6.3*
5.2, part	*6.4*
5.3	*6.5*
—	*6.6*
5.4	*6.7*
5.5	*6.8*
5.6	*6.9*
5.7	*6.10*
5.8	*6.11*
Transfer etc	
6	*7*
6.1	*7.1*
6.2	*7.2*
6.3	*7.3*
6.4	*7.4*